Writing Canadian English

A Beginning
Second Edition – Revised

Student Workbook

Sheridan Anderson
M. Elaine Sorensen

Detselig Enterprises Ltd.

Calgary, Alberta, Canada

Writing Canadian English: A Beginning – Student Workbook
© 1999 Detselig Enterprises Ltd.

Canadian Cataloguing in Publication Data

Anderson, Sheridan,
Writing Canadian English: a beginning. Student workbook

ISBN 1-55059-182-7

1. English language—Textbooks for second language learners.* 2. English language—Grammar—Problems, exercises, etc. 3. English language—Composition and exercises. I. Sorensen, M. Elaine (Marion Elaine), II. Title.

PE1128.A542 1999   428.2'4   C99-910184-6

Detselig Enterprises Ltd.
210-1220 Kensington Rd. N.W.
Calgary, Alberta T2N 3P5
Phone: (403) 283-0900/Fax: (403) 283-6947
e-mail: temeron@telusplanet.net
www.temerondetselig.com

Detselig Enterprises Ltd. appreciates the financial support for our 1999 publishing program, provided by Canadian Heritage and other sources.

Printed in Canada

ISBN 1-55059-182-7

SAN 115-0324

Cover design by Dean Macdonald

First edition 1981
Second printing 1988
Third printing 1993
Second edition 1999

Contents

Acknowledgements

We would like to express our thanks to the instructors and students who have used this material in one form or another, and especially to Jill Wyatt of the Calgary Board of Education and Dr. James Anderson of the University of Calgary for their advice and helpful comments and suggestions.

M.S.A.   M.E.S.

Unit I

To Be, Noun Plurals, Time

A. Rewrite the entire sentence, adding the correct form of the verb to be.

Example: She _____ a nurse.
She is a nurse.

1. We _____ friends. _____

2. They _____ here. _____

3. I _____ a student. _____

4. The dog _____ hungry. _____

5. Joseph _____ a Canadian. _____

6. You and Bill _____ friendly. _____

7. It _____ a nice day. _____

8. I _____ cold. _____

9. Sally _____ French. _____

10. Julie and Jill _____ sisters. _____

B. Rewrite the sentence in the interrogative.

Example: We are teachers.
Are we teachers?

1. I'm first. _____

2. She isn't Greek. _____

3. The house is big. _____

4. He isn't a doctor. _____

5. They're intelligent. _____

6. You aren't very pleased. _____

7. Robert is twenty-six. _____

8. The children are hungry. _____

9. Janice is sixteen. _____

10. We're busy tomorrow. _____

C. Rewrite the sentence in the negative.

1. You're the teacher. _____

2. I'm a lawyer. _____

3. The boys are there. _____

4. We're students. _____

5. It's a nice day. _____

6. They're Chinese. _____

7. Jeremy is thirsty. _____

8. Louis is from Quebec. _____

9. The women are busy. _____

10. She is young. _____

D. Answer the following questions. Use <u>yes</u> or <u>no</u> in your answer.

1. Are you a teacher? _____

2. Are you a good student? _____

3. Is the table red? _____

4. Are the chairs green? _____

5. Is there a window in the room? _____

_____

6. Are your shoes brown? _____

7. Is your teacher a man? _____

8. Are you Japanese? _____

9. Is your coat orange? _____

10. Is the sky blue today? _____

E. Change the underlined words to a pronoun.

Example: <u>John</u> *is an engineer.*
He is an engineer.

1. <u>The man</u> is old. _____

2. <u>The books</u> are on the table. _____

3. <u>The desk</u> isn't brown. _____

4. <u>The girl</u> is fifteen. _____

5. <u>The men</u> aren't friendly. _____

6. <u>John and I</u> are good friends. _____

7. <u>The chairs</u> are yellow. _____

8. <u>You and your sister</u> are Polish. _____

9. <u>Bob and Brian</u> are from England. _____

10. <u>Samuel and I</u> aren't hungry. _____

11. <u>The children</u> are young. _____

12. <u>The house</u> is green. _____

13. <u>Mr. and Mrs. Stevens</u> are American. _____

14. <u>You and I</u> aren't clever students. _____

15. <u>The doctor</u> is a busy woman. _____

16. <u>The sheep</u> are in the field. _____

17. <u>You and your friends</u> are in the wrong room. _____

_____

18. <u>The dog and the cat</u> are the same age. _____

19. <u>The professor</u> is a nice lady. _____

20. <u>The sheep</u> is woolly. _____

F. Rewrite the following paragraph, changing <u>Maria</u> to <u>Jack</u>. Make any other changes necessary.

This is Maria. She is a student. She is friendly and she's intelligent. She's Spanish. She is seventeen.

_____

_____

_____

Change <u>Robert</u> to <u>Marianne</u>.

This is Robert. He isn't a teacher. He's an engineer. He is French. Today he is not well. He is sick.

_____

_____

_____

Change <u>Miss Brunet</u> to <u>I</u>.

Miss Brunet is a teacher. She isn't a nurse. She is Canadian and she is from Quebec. She is friendly and nice. Miss Brunet is young. She is twenty-two.

_____

_____

_____

_____

G. Fill in the blanks with <u>a</u>, <u>an</u> or <u>x</u> (<u>x</u> means no article is required).

1. You are not _____ teachers.

2. They are _____ young.

3. I am _____ student.

4. He is _____ French.

5. We are not _____ doctors.

6. You are _____ Chilean.

7. I am _____ twenty-five.

8. Mr. and Mrs. Andrews are _____ Canadian.

9. You are _____ busy woman.

10. Mary is _____ Japanese.

11. We are _____ friends.

12. Robert isn't _____ young.

13. He is _____ young musician.

14. She is _____ good lawyer.

15. You are _____ electrician.

H. Rewrite the sentence with plural subjects.

1. I am a teacher. _____

2. You are a good student. _____

3. She is hungry. _____

4. He is a businessman. _____

5. It is a shoe. _____

6. The child is busy. _____

7. It is a pencil, not a pen. _____

I. Rewrite the sentences with a singular subject.

1. We're not children. _____

2. You are friendly and nice. _____

3. They are good doctors. _____

4. They are twenty-two. _____

5. We are Spanish. _____

6. The girls are at home. _____

7. Policemen aren't small. _____

J. Telling time.

What time is it?

It is ten past one
(ten after one).

It is one o'clock.

It is half past one
(one-thirty).

It is a quarter past one
(quarter after one).

It is a quarter to eleven
(ten forty-five).

It is twenty-five to
eleven (ten thirty-five).

It is twelve o'clock
(noon, midnight).

It is five to eleven
(ten fifty-five).

What time is it?

Model Composition

Geography of Canada

Canada is about 5514 km wide. The Atlantic Ocean is on the east coast and the Pacific Ocean is on the west. The United States is to the south. The Rockies are the most important mountains of Canada and they are in the provinces of Alberta and British Columbia.

There are many important rivers in this country, including the St. Lawrence in the east, the Fraser and Thompson rivers in the west, the Mackenzie in the north and the Saskatchewan in the central part of the country.

There are ten provinces and three territories in Canada: British Columbia, Alberta, Saskatchewan, Manitoba, Ontario, Quebec, New Brunswick, Nova Scotia, Prince Edward Island, Newfoundland, Northwest Territories, the Yukon Territory and Nunavut, which became a territory in 1999. The capital of Canada is Ottawa.

The population is about 29 million people, and the two official languages are English and French.

Questions:

1. How wide is Canada? _____

2. What is on the east coast? _____

_____

3. What is on the west coast? _____

_____

4. What country is to the south of Canada? _____

_____

5. What are the most important mountains? _____

_____

6. Where are the Rockies? _____

_____

7. What are some of the most important rivers? _____

_____

_____

_____

8. How many provinces and territories are there in Canada? _____

_____

9. What is the population of Canada? _____

_____

10. What are the two official languages? _____

_____

MAP

Write a composition about <u>your</u> country, following the model.

_____

_____

_____

_____

_____

_____

_____

_____

_____

_____

_____

_____

_____

_____

_____

_____

_____

_____

_____

_____

_____

_____

Unit II

Simple Present, Object Pronouns

A. Write the third person singular form of each of the following verbs:

Example: *move*
           he moves

1. have _____
2. do _____
3. say _____
4. ask _____
5. come _____

6. go _____
7. dry _____
8. write _____
9. play _____
10. study _____

B. Rewrite the sentence, adding the correct form of the verb in parentheses.

1. He (walk) to school at eight o'clock. _____

_____

2. Mrs. Jones (wash) clothes on Mondays. _____

_____

3. I (eat) lunch at noon. _____

4. The dogs (chase) the cats. _____

5. We (learn) new words every day. _____

_____

6. The bird (fly) over the house. _____

7. The boy (catch) a cold every spring. _____

_____

8. The women (study) in the library on Wednesdays. _____

_____

9. Marilyn (do) her homework in the evening. _____

_____

10. Mr. Brown (wash) the windows once a week. _____

_____

C. Rewrite the paragraph, adding the correct form of the required verbs. Use each verb only once.

Mrs. Andrews _____ a housewife. She _____ eight children. She _____ very hard at home. On Monday mornings she _____ clothes. She _____ them on Tuesdays. Wednesdays she _____ bread, pie and cookies. She _____ the house every Thursday. On Fridays she _____ a holiday and _____ at home. She _____ until noon, then _____ television. Friday night, Mr. Andrews _____ supper for the children. After supper they all _____ to the movies.

	bake	be	clean	cook	go	have
iron	relax	sleep	take	wash	watch	work

_____

_____

_____

_____

_____

_____

_____

_____

_____

_____

_____

D. Rewrite the paragraph, changing I to Robert.

I like sports! I live in British Columbia near mountains and lakes. In the summer I swim and golf. When friends come to visit I like to play tennis or walk with them. In the winter I skate and ski. Once a week I curl with my family. Sometimes in the evenings I watch football or hockey games on television.

_____

_____

_____

_____

_____

_____

_____

E. Read the paragraph, then rewrite, changing I to The men.

I go to work every day at nine. I work in an office. I work with machines and numbers. I am an accountant.

_____

_____

_____

Write a similar paragraph to the above using the following information:

Jane   seven   animal clinic   sick dogs and cats   veterinarian

_____

_____

_____

F. Rewrite the sentence, choosing the correct pronoun.

1. She writes (I, me) a letter once a month. _____

_____

2. I ski with (he, him) every Saturday. _____

_____

3. We see (they, them) on Tuesdays. _____

4. John and (he, him) walk to school every morning. _____

_____

5. The boys speak to (she, her) in class. _____

_____

6. I understand (they, them) very well. _____

_____

7. Mary and (I, me) like to play golf. _____

_____

8. The white dog chases (we, us). _____

9. The letter is from (I, me). _____

10. You and (I, me) are friends. _____

11. He and (I, me) work together every afternoon. _____

_____

12. John asks (she, her) a question. _____

G. Rewrite each sentence, changing underlined words to pronouns.

1. <u>John</u> sees <u>Mary</u>. _____

2. <u>The students</u> play football with <u>Mr. Jones</u>. _____

_____

3. <u>The boy</u> likes <u>the book</u>. _____

4. <u>The women</u> give clothes to <u>the children</u>. _____

5. The teacher gives <u>the students and me</u> the homework. _____

_____

6. <u>Bob</u> sits in front of <u>you and me</u>. _____

7. We are friends with <u>Bill and Ruth</u>. _____

8. I live in Montreal and I like <u>Montreal</u>. _____

_____

9. Jane studies French and <u>Jane</u> like <u>French</u>. _____

_____

10. I like Susan and Jim and I see <u>Susan and Jim</u> once a week. _____

_____

11. We know Robert and we understand <u>Robert</u>. _____

_____

H. Change the order of the direct and indirect objects, then change the nouns to pronouns.

Example: I tell Bob the answers.
I tell the answers to Bob.
I tell them to him.

1. She gives Judy the red shoes. _____

_____

2. The father lends his son the purple coat. _____

_____

3. Mrs. Kelly takes the boys the pie. _____

_____

4. The businessman gives the accountant the numbers. _____

_____

_____

5. The teacher tells the children a story. _____

Model Composition

Leisure Time in Canada

Canadians spend their leisure time in many different ways. On weekends some go to the mountains to ski or hike. Others prefer to stay in town and meet at the ice-rink or to watch ice-hockey. In the evenings many people like to visit the curling rink or go to a movie.

On their vacations, a lot of Canadians enjoy visiting the many national parks in their country. The beautiful beaches of British Columbia, Nova Scotia and Prince Edward Island have many visitors each year.

Other sports enjoyed by Canadians are tennis, swimming, snowshoeing, canoeing, lacrosse, in-line skating and golf.

Questions:

1. How do some Canadians spend their weekends? _____

_____

_____

_____

2. What do many people like to visit in the evenings? _____

_____

3. What do a lot of Canadians do on their vacations? _____

_____

4. What beaches have many visitors each year? _____

_____

_____

5. What are some other sports enjoyed by Canadians? _____

_____

_____

Write a composition about leisure time in your country, following the model.

_____

_____

_____

_____

_____

_____

_____

_____

_____

Unit III

Simple Present (cont.), Possessive Adjectives/Pronouns

A. Write the sentence in the interrogative.

1. He plays the piano well. _____

2. You buy skates in a sports store. _____

_____

3. The children love their parents. _____

_____

4. The mail comes at nine o'clock. _____

_____

5. Christmas Day comes on December 25th. _____

_____

6. The television stands on the floor. _____

_____

7. We swim every week. _____

8. I buy my clothes in a department store. _____

_____

9. Miss Conrad asks me questions. _____

_____

10. You know the answers. _____

11. Women like candy and flowers. _____

_____

B. Write the sentence in the negative.

1. We skate on the lake in the winter. _____

_____

2. I ski in the mountains on my holidays. _____

_____

3. Charles buys a new car every spring. _____

_____

4. They move to a new city every fall. _____

_____

5. Judy swims with her friends. _____

_____

6. You often buy your parents presents. _____

_____

7. We visit the library every evening. _____

_____

8. Mr. Roche celebrates his birthday every July. _____

_____

9. The airplanes fly over my house. _____

_____

10. Canadians observe many holidays every year. _____

_____

11. Men cook very well. _____

12. The little girl plays with her toys every morning. _____

_____

C. Read the following paragraph, then answer the questions in complete sentences.

Sally Martin is from the United States. She speaks English and Spanish. She works in an office. Sally is a secretary. She writes letters, takes the mail to the boss and answers the telephone. She goes to work at nine o'clock and comes home at five o'clock, five days a week. On Saturdays and Sundays she relaxes at home or visits her friends.

1. Is Sally from the United States? _____

_____

2. Does she speak English and Spanish? _____

_____

3. Does she speak Russian? _____

4. Does she work in an office? _____

5. Is she an accountant? _____

6. Does she write letters at work? _____

_____

7. Does she take coffee to the boss? _____

_____

8. Does she go to work at eight o'clock? _____

_____

9. Does she come home at five o'clock? _____

_____

10. Does she work seven days a week? _____

_____

11. Does she visit friends on Saturdays and Sundays? _____

_____

12. Does she relax at the office on Saturdays and Sundays? _____

_____

Rewrite the entire paragraph in the negative.

_____

_____

_____

_____

_____

_____

_____

D. Write a paragraph by answering each question in the affirmative. Do not use _yes_.

Does Beatrice like to take a holiday? Does she visit her friends in Spain? Do they live in a city in the south? Is it always hot in the winter there? Does Beatrice swim in the lakes and hike in the mountains? Does she go to the movies in the evenings? Does she always have a good time with her friends?

_____

_____

_____

_____

_____

_____

_____

E. Rewrite the sentence in the interrogative.

1. We don't ask questions in an exam. _____

2. Mary walks home every evening. _____

_____

3. The cat doesn't like dogs. _____

4. They buy lunch at school. _____

5. I am hungry. _____

6. Jim writes his friend a letter every week. _____

_____

7. You're tired today. _____

8. The teachers have a good time at school. _____

_____

9. I take the bus downtown today. _____

10. It isn't Thursday. _____

11. The grandparents watch television at night. _____

_____

12. We have supper at six o'clock. _____

13. Victoria Day is in May. _____

F. Form three questions for each short answer.

Example: *Yes, he is.*   *(a) Is he a doctor?*
                                 (b) Is he from Quebec?
                                 (c) Is he your friend?

1. Yes, I am.   (a) _____

                      (b) _____

                      (c) _____

2. No, we aren't.   (a) _____

                      (b) _____

                      (c) _____

3. Yes, they do.   (a) _____

                      (b) _____

                      (c) _____

4. Yes, it is.   (a) _____

                      (b) _____

(c) _____

5. No, she doesn't.   (a) _____

(b) _____

(c) _____

G. Rewrite the sentences as in the following example.

Example: The book belongs to me. (a) It is my book.
(b) It is mine.

1. The car belongs to him.   (a) _____

(b) _____

2. The watches belong to you.   (a) _____

(b) _____

3. The cat belongs to Judy.   (a) _____

(b) _____

4. The television belongs to them. (a) _____

(b) _____

5. The jewelry belongs to her.   (a) _____

(b) _____

6. The beautiful clothes belong to us. (a) _____

(b) _____

7. The letters belong to Bob.   (a) _____

(b) _____

8. The bird belongs to me.   (a) _____

(b) _____

9. The house belongs to you and me. (a) _____

(b) _____

H. Answer the following questions affirmatively, using a possessive adjective or possessive pronoun where possible.

1. Is it his dog? _____

2. Are they my shoes? _____

3. Is Miriam her sister? _____

4. Do you see its bone? _____

5. Do we know our teacher? _____

6. Does she like your brother? _____

7. Do they visit their friends? _____

8. Is it his lunch? _____

9. Do they write to their parents? _____

10. Are we her students? _____

11. Does it eat its food? _____

12. Is she your mother? _____

13. Do you like my blue car? _____

I. Read the following paragraph.

I am a busy student. My teachers ask me questions every day in class. I study my textbooks. They are mine.

Now rewrite the paragraph with the following changes:
1. Change I to He.
2. Change I to They.

_____

_____

_____

_____

_____

_____

J. Rewrite the following sentences adding a possessive adjective.

Example: *We eat lunch at nine.*
We eat our lunch at nine.

1. She buys new shoes at the department store. _____

_____

2. The students talk to friends. _____

_____

3. I wash walls once a week. _____

4. We walk to school every day. _____

5. He eats supper at six o'clock. _____

_____

6. You and I speak English at home. _____

_____

7. You do homework every night. _____

_____

8. John and I go to the movies with friends. _____

_____

9. Sally and Bill have classes with Mr. Johnson. _____

_____

10. You and he take coffee black. _____

_____

K. Model Composition

The Weather

There are four seasons in Calgary: spring, summer, autumn and winter. In spring it is very pleasant and the plants and trees begin to grow. The summer is hot and dry and often it is very windy. The autumn is sometimes called "fall" because it is the time when the leaves fall from the trees. The winter in Calgary is usually very cold but the sky is clear and blue. Sometimes the Chinook winds blow from the west bringing warm days and melting the snow.

sun   cool   rain   sunny   mild   cold   wet   rainy   warm   freezing
humid   windy   hot   wind   hail   cloudy   dry   snow   cloud   ice

Write a short composition about the weather in your country, following the model above.

_____

_____

_____

_____

_____

_____

_____

_____

_____

_____

Model Composition

Legal Holidays

January 1st is New Year's Day and it is the first holiday of the year. Next comes Good Friday. It is the Friday before Easter and it usually falls in April. The first Monday before May 25 is Victoria Day. This is celebrated in all provinces except Quebec. July 1st is Canada Day, which is the anniversary of Confederation. Labour Day is the first Monday in September. In October we celebrate Thanksgiving when we give thanks for the harvest. November 11th is Remembrance Day. We remember the men who died in the World Wars on this day. The last holiday of the year is Christmas on December 25th.

In addition, Canadians observe several holidays unofficially. Among these are St. Valentine's Day for love on February 14th, and April Fools' Day on April 1st. Finally, Hallowe'en is October 31st, the eve of All Saints Day, when the children dress up and put on masks.

Questions:

1. What is the first holiday of the year? _____

_____

2. When is Good Friday? _____

_____

3. When is Victoria Day? _____

_____

4. What falls on July 1st? _____

_____

5. When is Labour Day? _____

_____

6. When do we give thanks for the harvest? _____

_____

7. When is Remembrance Day? _____

_____

8. What is the last holiday of the year? _____

_____

9. What are some of the days Canadians observe unofficially? _____

_____

Write a composition about the holidays in <u>your</u> country, following the model.

_____

_____

_____

_____

_____

_____

_____

_____

_____

_____

_____

_____

_____

_____

_____

_____

_____

_____

_____

_____

_____

_____

_____

_____

_____

Crossword Puzzle

ACROSS
1. We _____ students.
3. Opposite of come.
5. Put the book _____ the table.
6. _____ is cold outside.
8. Opposite of happy.
10. Ottawa is the capital _____ Canada.
11. He is _____ doctor.
12. Simple (base) form of does.
14. One color of the Canadian flag.
17. Possessive pronoun.
18. Subject pronoun.

DOWN
1. I _____ Canadian.
2. He usually _____ a big dinner.
3. Opposite of bad.
4. I go to school _____ Tuesdays.
7. My name is Joe. What's _____ name?
9. Nineteen hundred _____ seventy-nine.
13. Possessive pronoun.
15. If you want to see, you need at least one _____.
16. How _____ you like Canada?

Unit IV

Present Progressive, Reflexive Pronouns

A. Change <u>every day</u> to <u>now</u>. Remember to change the verb from the simple present tense to the present progressive tense.

Example: I exercise every day.
I am exercising now.

1. I sleep every day. _____

2. He sits in the cafeteria every day. _____

_____

3. The children talk to their mother every day. _____

_____

4. We wait for her every day. _____

5. It snows every day. _____

6. You study English every day. _____

7. The policemen help people every day. _____

_____

8. I teach them mathematics every day. _____

_____

9. The sun shines every day. _____

10. You work hard every day. _____

11. The baby sleeps every day. _____

B. Rewrite the sentences in the negative.

1. I'm going home at five o'clock. _____

_____

2. You are enjoying the movie. _____

_____

3. She is helping her friend now. _____

_____

4. I am washing the dishes at this moment. _____

_____

5. We're studying English at present. _____

6. Joseph is cooking dinner right now. _____

_____

7. You and I are listening to the teacher. _____

_____

8. The dogs are chasing the cats. _____

_____

9. Miss Bennett is speaking French now. _____

_____

10. They're flying to Europe next week. _____

_____

C. Rewrite the sentences in the interrogative.

1. You are eating my lunch. _____

2. Bob and Juan are going to the concert. _____

_____

3. I'm writing a letter now. _____

4. The boss is listening to the secretary. _____

_____

5. We are watching television right now. _____

_____

6. Margarita is waiting for the teacher. _____

_____

7. They are coming here tomorrow. _____

_____

8. The cat is sleeping by the fire. _____

_____

9. You're having a test next week. _____

_____

10. I'm sitting in my office at present. _____

_____

D. Rewrite the following paragraph, adding the present progressive form of the required verbs. Use each verb only once.

It is autumn. The leaves _____ yellow and orange and _____ to the ground. A cold wind _____. The days _____ shorter.

People _____ for Thanksgiving. Fathers _____ vegetables from the gardens. Mothers _____ turkeys and _____ pumpkin pies. Children _____ in the leaves. Animals are busy too. They _____ food for the winter. Many birds _____ south.

bake   blow   cook   fall   fly   get   play   prepare   store   turn   gather

_____

_____

_____

_____

_____

_____

_____

_____

_____

_____

_____

E. Make three questions for each answer. Include a verb in the present progressive tense in each question.

Example: *Yes, I am. (a) Are you eating lunch now?*
(b) Are you writing a letter?
(c) Are you leaving?

1. No, he isn't.   (a) _____

(b) _____

(c) _____

2. Yes, you are.   (a) _____

(b) _____

(c) _____

3. No, they aren't.   (a) _____

(b) _____

(c) _____

F. Answer the following questions in complete sentences.

1. Are you getting cold? _____

2. Is it raining? _____

3. Is your teacher sitting? _____

4. Are the students sleeping now? _____

_____

5. Are you studying French now? _____

_____

6. Is the sun shining? _____

7. Is your friend wearing shoes? _____

_____

8. Are you listening to the teacher? _____

_____

9. Are you having a test next week? _____

_____

10. Is it snowing now? _____

G. Put the verb in parentheses in the present progressive or simple present tense as required.

1. You (read) a lot? What you (read) now? _____

_____

2. The moon (shine) at night. The moon (shine) now? _____

_____

3. It (snow) in winter. It (snow) now? _____

_____

4. Lorna (play) tennis well. She (play) this afternoon? _____

_____

5. Carlos (speak) Spanish. _____

6. Why you (take) off your shoes? I (go) to bed. _____

_____

7. She (not have) a baby. She only (appear) pregnant. _____

_____

8. What you (wear) today? _____

9. Margaret always (talk) so loud. _____

10. You (love) Don? No. I (like) him a lot but I (not love) him. _____

_____

11. Where is Jim? He (have) a shower. _____

12. It (rain) now? No, the sun (shine) and the birds (sing). _____

_____

H. Write a composition by answering the following questions affirmatively.

Are you studying English in Alberta? Are you going to college in a large city? Are you learning about the geography, history and customs of Canada?

Are you planning to stay in Alberta for several years? Are you trying to find a job? Are you making friends with Albertans and getting to know the country? Are you learning to ski and curl and are you getting used to the winter months?

Is your family coming to see you soon? Are you preparing for their visit? Are you waiting impatiently for their arrival? Are you planning to show them the beautiful country and introduce them to your friends?

_____

_____

_____

_____

_____

_____

_____

_____

_____

_____

_____

_____

_____

_____

_____

_____

_____

_____

_____

I. Read the following paragraph and write three similar ones using the information given below.

Joe is a mechanic. He usually works in a garage. Today he is working in a school. He is teaching the students how to fix cars.

1. Susan – nurse – hospital – factory – employees – prevent disease

_____

_____

_____

_____

2. I – teacher – school – office – secretaries – read French

_____

_____

_____

3. We – accountants – offices – department stores – salesmen – balance books

_____

_____

_____

_____

J. Move the object pronoun or noun to the front of the sentence and include a reflexive pronoun as in the example.

Example: Nobody cut him on the face.
He cut himself on the face.

1. Nobody helps us in a cafeteria. _____

_____

2. Nobody washes a cat. _____

3. Nobody entertains you at home. _____

_____

4. Nobody teaches them the lessons. _____

_____

5. Nobody helps me. _____

6. Nobody makes her the cake. _____

_____

7. Nobody hurts the child. _____

8. Nobody dries me after my bath. _____

_____

K. Rewrite the sentences, changing alone to by plus a reflexive pronoun.

Example: I watch television alone.
I watch television by myself.

1. I eat lunch alone. _____

2. You are going to the park alone. _____

_____

3. I'm listening to the music alone. _____

_____

4. He studies his lessons alone. _____

5. Paul walks to school alone. _____

_____

6. You sit alone. _____

7. She is cleaning the house alone. _____

_____

8. The cat sleeps alone. _____

9. Maria is going to the library alone. _____

_____

10. The dog is eating a bone alone. _____

_____

L. Read the following paragraph.

Eileen gets up at noon every day. She washes herself then dresses herself. She makes herself breakfast. She eats by herself. At one o'clock she drives herself to work.

1. Rewrite the paragraph, changing Eileen to I.

_____

_____

_____

_____

2. Rewrite the paragraph, changing Eileen to they.

_____

_____

_____

_____

Model Composition

National Parks

Canada covers more than half the continent of North America. Many areas in this large country are now national parks where the plants and wildlife are protected by the Government to preserve these regions in their natural state for all people to see and enjoy. In the parks there is beautiful scenery, great wilderness areas and many different kinds of animal life.

Each park is different from the rest, but in each one you can walk along nature trails with a guide, attend free evening talks and see exhibits.

There are about twenty-eight national parks in Canada today. Banff, Alberta, is the oldest.

Questions:

1. How much of North America does Canada cover? _____

_____

2. What are many areas in the country now? _____

_____

3. What does the Government do? _____

_____

4. What is there to see in the parks? _____

_____

5. What is there to do in the parks? _____

_____

6. About how many national parks are there in Canada today? _____

_____

7. Which park is the oldest? _____

_____

Write a composition about national parks in your country, following the model.

_____

_____

_____

_____

_____

_____

_____

_____

_____

Unit V

Past Tense <u>To Be</u>, Regular Verbs, Demonstratives

A. Rewrite each of the sentences to show that the action occurred in the past.

Example: I walk to school every day.
I walked to school yesterday.

1. Robert lives in Quebec. _____

2. The dog follows the children everywhere. _____

_____

3. Marilyn needs a new coat. _____

4. The students arrive at school at eight every day. _____

_____

5. I play tennis every Saturday at eleven forty-five. _____

_____

6. You clean the house every week. _____

7. His lesson ends at three o'clock. _____

8. Colin visits his family every Christmas. _____

_____

9. We listen to the radio every morning. _____

_____

10. I am hungry this afternoon. _____

11. The men attend the conference every year. _____

_____

12. You open the window at night. _____

_____

13. She washes her hair once a week. _____

_____

14. We learn many new words each day. _____

_____

15. I carry her books home every night. _____

_____

16. The children want to go to the movies. _____

17. I use my dictionary every day. _____

18. Joan changes her clothes every day. _____

19. We always try to speak English in class. _____

20. The teacher spells the new words. _____

21. The children play at the beach in summer. _____

22. She shows me her work after supper. _____

23. We hurry home from work. _____

B. Fill in the blanks with a verb from the list in the past tense.

1. She _____ herself a cup of coffee.

2. The student _____ the teacher some questions.

3. My mother _____ bread yesterday.

4. The bread _____ delicious.

5. The movie _____ at midnight.

6. The family _____ in Vancouver for three weeks last summer.

7. Last winter it _____ a great deal in Canada.

8. Jack _____ for the city last year.

9. The lecture _____ two hours yesterday.

10. The cashier _____ the money very carefully.

    ask   bake   count   end   last   pour   smell   snow   stay   work

C. Answer each question negatively. Then give an affirmative answer using the word in parentheses.

Example: *Were you a student in Australia? (Canada)*
           No, I wasn't a student in Australia.
           I was a student in Canada.

1. Was he your boss? (teacher) _____

2. Were they the third group of students? (second) _____

_____

_____

3. Was that man you uncle? (father) _____

_____

4. Was the book interesting? (boring) _____

_____

5. Were you in Winnipeg on October 10th? (Toronto) _____

_____

_____

6. Was I early for class yesterday? (late) _____

_____

7. Was Theresa at your house on January 5th? (office) _____

_____

_____

8. Were they Japanese? (Korean) _____

_____

9. Was the dog yours? (Robert's) _____

_____

10. Were they his neighbors? (classmates) _____

_____

D. Fill in the blanks.

1. Mary usually cooks supper at five, but last night she _____ it at six.

2. He usually prepares his lessons at night, but yesterday he _____ them in the morning.

3. We usually visit our friends on Saturdays, but last week we _____ them on Sunday.

4. It usually snows in October, but last year it _____ in August.

5. He usually washes his car once a week, but last week he _____ it every day.

6. I usually study in the afternoons, but yesterday I _____ in the evening.

7. You usually arrive at school on time, but yesterday you _____ late.

8. The men usually pay their bills on Fridays, but last week they _____ on Thursday.

9. I usually carry Sherry's books to school, but last month I _____ Alice's books.

10. John and I usually answer the students' questions, but yesterday we _____ the teacher's questions.

E. Rewrite the following paragraph, adding the correct form of the verbs in parentheses.

Last week-end I _____ (visit) some old friends in the country. I _____ (arrive) at their farm Friday evening. That evening we _____ (talk) and _____ (joke) about old times. The next morning we _____ (walk) around the farm and _____ (look) at the animals. In the afternoon I _____ (help) my friends in their garden. We _____ (attend) a barn dance that evening. My friends _____ (introduce) me to the neighbors who _____ (be) there. I _____ (dance) with everyone. I _____ (try) to do all the old-fashioned dances but sometimes I _____ (stop) and just _____ (listen) to the music. The next day I _____ (be) very tired and I _____ (want) to stay longer. But, I _____ (hurry) back to the city in order to avoid the week-end rush traffic.

_____

_____

_____

_____

_____

_____

_____

_____

_____

_____

_____

_____

_____

_____

_____

_____

_____

_____

_____

F. Rewrite the following paragraph, changing <u>every day</u> to <u>yesterday</u>.

Susan hurries home from school every day at four o'clock. She quickly changes her clothes and grabs something to eat. Then, she waits for the bus outside. The bus stops in front of her house. Susan climbs into the bus and it carries her downtown. She steps off the bus in front of the Bay. She walks to the drugstore where she works. At five-thirty she starts her job. She washes the floors, cleans the counters and empties the garbage. She finishes work at eight o'clock. She is very tired and returns home by bus.

_____

_____

_____

_____

_____

_____

_____

_____

_____

_____

_____

G. Read the following paragraph.

This is my friend. He lives in that house over there. He is a salesman. That blue car is his.

1. Rewrite in the plural.

_____

_____

2. Rewrite in the interrogative.

_____

_____

H. Rewrite, inserting <u>one</u> or <u>ones</u> where possible.

Example: I have a dog and my friend has a dog.
I have a dog and my friend has one.

Bill likes to be different. His father has a new car but Bill has an old car. His mother likes tidy rooms but Bill likes messy rooms. His brother wears blue jeans but Bill wears black jeans. His friend has a beard but Bill doesn't have a beard. His girl friend wants a wedding but Bill doesn't want a wedding.

_____

_____

_____

_____

_____

_____

I. Write each sentence in the plural.

1. This is my first car. _____

2. That was a bird. _____

3. That man is my friend. _____

4. This is the teacher. _____

5. Is that a mouse? _____

6. This wasn't a good lesson. _____

7. This coat isn't hers, but that one is. _____
   _____

8. This woman speaks French. _____

9. Wasn't this book yours? _____

10. That child doesn't like milk but this one does. _____
    _____

J. Write each sentence in the singular.

1. These are new teeth. _____

2. Those weren't the questions. _____

3. Do these shoes fit you? _____

4. Those people come from Nova Scotia. _____
   _____

5. Aren't these your pencils? _____

6. Don't those students do their work? _____
   _____

7. Those are American teachers. _____

8. Don't these offices have chairs? _____

9. We remember these lessons, but we don't remember those. _____
   _____

10. I like these hats but I don't like those. _____
    _____

Family Ties

Maxwell Anderson (retired) = **Virginia** (retired)

Gordon Anderson (building contractor) = **Anne**

James Anderson (university professor) = **Sherry** (English teacher)

Robert Anderson (fireman) = **Geri**

Christine (supervisor, airplane manufacturer)
Cynthia (restaurant manager)
Wendy (university student)
Keith (high school student)
Maren (jr. high school student)

Siwan (high school student)
Corri (elementary school student)

Kim (high school student)
Mark (jr. high school student)

My husband's family is large. His parents are retired and live in the country. He has two brothers and both of them are married. Gordon builds houses and he has five children. He and his wife Anne live near the sea.

Robert, who we call Bob, is a fireman and he lives in town with his wife Geri and their daughter, Kim, and their son, Mark.

My husband and I have two children also: a girl, Siwan, who attends Branton Junior High School, and a son, Corri, who goes to the elementary school. We live in Calgary. Last of all there is our dog, Mumbles, who is also an important member of our family.

1. What relation is Maxwell Anderson to Gordon Anderson? _____

_____

to Geri Anderson? _____

to Corri Anderson? _____

2. What relation is Sherry Anderson to Anne Anderson? _____

_____

to Siwan Anderson? _____

to Christine Anderson? _____

to Virginia Anderson? _____

3. What relation is Robert Anderson to James Anderson? _____

_____

to Maren Anderson? _____

to Anne Anderson? _____

to Kim Anderson? _____

4. What relation is Wendy Anderson to Kim and Mark Anderson? _____

_____

to Sherry Anderson? _____

to Virginia Anderson? _____

Write a short composition describing your family following the model above.

_____

_____

_____

_____

_____

_____

_____

_____

_____

_____

_____

_____

_____

_____

_____

_____

_____

Model Composition

Settlers from Overseas

The ancestors of most Canadians sailed from Britain in the 17th century. In addition, many people came from France and settled in an area called New France, later named Quebec. There were several wars between the French and English, but in 1763 France signed an agreement that New France belonged to Britain. The French Canadians were allowed to keep most of their laws, their religion and their language.

In 1781, the Americans gained their independence, but about forty thousand of them who wanted to remain British arrived in Canada to stay.

By 1791, Quebec was divided into Upper Canada and Lower Canada with an elected assembly in each.

On July 1, 1867, Canada became a Dominion and on that day, Sir John A. MacDonald became Prime Minister. He wanted Canada to reach from the Atlantic to the Pacific, and in 1885 the railway was completed from east to west. At that time many new settlers arrived from Britain, Scandinavia, Russia, Poland, Germany, Austria, the Ukraine and Italy. Life was very hard for these people at first.

Questions:

1. Who sailed to Canada in the 17th century? _____

_____

2. Who settled in New France? _____

_____

3. What happened in 1763? in 1781? in 1791? _____

_____

_____

_____

4. When did Canada become a Dominion? _____

_____

5. What did Sir John A. MacDonald want? _____

_____

6. Where did the new settlers come from? _____

_____

7. Can you think of any other groups of people who have settled in Canada? _____

_____

_____

Unit VI

Past Tense Regular Verbs (cont.), <u>There is</u>, <u>There are</u>, <u>Can</u>

A. **Rewrite each of the following sentences in the interrogative.**
Rewrite each of the following sentences, changing the verb to the past
tense. Change the time or frequency phrase to <u>yesterday</u>.
Rewrite each of your past tense sentences in the interrogative.

Example: *I wash the dishes every day.*
Do you wash the dishes every day?
I washed the dishes yesterday.
Did you wash the dishes yesterday?

1. I am sleepy today. _____

_____

_____

2. We try to speak English in class every day. _____

_____

_____

_____

3. They are in the country today. _____

_____

_____

4. The boy kicks the football every day. _____

_____

_____

_____

5. The dogs walk in the park every day. _____

_____

_____

_____

6. It is my turn today. _____

_____

_____

7. You clean your room every day. _____

_____

_____

8. We play cards every day. _____

_____

_____

9. The boys watch the girls every day. _____

_____

_____

_____

B. Rewrite each of following sentences in the negative.
Then rewrite each of the following sentences, changing the verb to the
past tense and changing the time or frequency phrase to <u>last week</u>.
Rewrite each of your past tense sentences in the negative.

Example: *He walks to school every day.*
He doesn't walk to school every day.
He walked to school last week.
He didn't walk to school last week.

1. He smokes a pipe in the evenings. _____

_____

_____

2. We talk to our friends every day. _____

_____

_____

3. They are in Paris this week. _____

_____

_____

4. It snows a lot every year. _____

_____

_____

5. I am sick today. _____

_____

_____

6. She pays me fifty dollars every week. _____

_____

_____

_____

7. The milkman calls at my house every morning. _____

_____

_____

_____

8. You are a good student today. _____

_____

_____

9. They say good morning to me every day. _____

_____

_____

_____

C. Answer each question negatively; then, write an affirmative answer using the information in parentheses.

Example: Did she cook supper yesterday? (breakfast)
No, she didn't cook supper yesterday.
She cooked breakfast yesterday.

1. Did he visit her last night? (them) _____

_____

2. Did you clean your room? (desk) _____

_____

3. Did we finish the book? (chapter) _____

_____

4. Did I pay the milkman? (paperboy) _____

_____

5. Did Jean study the lesson? (notes) _____

_____

6. Did you open the window? (door) _____

_____

7. Did they watch the news? (late movie) _____

_____

8. Did Andrew say hello? (goodbye) _____

9. Did the girls remember the accident? (policeman) _____

_____

10. Did we listen to the radio last night? (stereo) _____

_____

D. Write three questions for each answer.

    Example: *Yes, I do.*   *(a) Do you speak English?*
                                    (b) Do you like Canada?
                                    (c) Do you walk to school?

1. Yes, you did.   (a) _____
                      (b) _____
                      (c) _____

2. No, they aren't.   (a) _____
                      (b) _____
                      (c) _____

3. Yes, we do.   (a) _____
                      (b) _____
                      (c) _____

4. Yes, I was.   (a) _____
                      (b) _____
                      (c) _____

5. No, she didn't.   (a) _____
                      (b) _____
                      (c) _____

E. Write three paragraphs by answering the following questions affirmatively. (Do not write <u>yes</u>).

    Was yesterday a beautiful day? Did Sally decide to take the morning off work? Did she dress before breakfast and telephone her friend Anne? After breakfast, did she walk to the corner to meet Anne? Did they stop a taxi and ask the driver to take them to the zoo? Did they arrive at the zoo before the gates opened? Did they wait for ten minutes until nine o'clock? Did they pay $3 when they returned?

    Were there many animals to see? Did they watch the monkeys for a while, then walk over to the bear cages? Did they listen to the noisy bears? Were the lions next to the bears? Did a big lion show the girls his teeth? Did the girls stay only a short time by his cage? Did they notice a kangaroo in a large pen? Did it carry its baby in a pouch?

Were Sally and Anne sorry to leave the zoo? Did they finally remember their jobs? Did they rush away at noon to find a bus?

_____

_____

_____

_____

_____

_____

_____

_____

_____

_____

_____

_____

_____

_____

_____

_____

_____

_____

_____

F. Write sentences using the given words. Include a <u>there</u> in each sentence.

Example: *book / desk*
          There is a book on the desk.

1. pen/drawer _____

2. clothes/closet _____

3. not/students/classroom _____

_____

4. not/coffee/coffee pot _____

5. orange/refrigerator _____

6. dog/park _____

7. not/paper/notebook _____

8. bone/dog's mouth _____

9. not/cookies/bag _____

10. not/leaves/tree _____

G. Answer the following questions in complete sentences.

1. How many days are there in a week? _____

_____

2. How many provinces are there in Canada? _____

_____

3. How many students are there in the class? _____

_____

4. How many windows are there in the classroom? _____

_____

5. How many Italians are there in the class? _____

_____

6. How many weeks are there in a year? _____

_____

7. How many watches are there on your arm? _____

_____

8. How many months are there in a year? _____

_____

9. How many rings are there on your fingers? _____

_____

10. How many English teachers are there in the room? _____

_____

H. Change the underlined part of the sentence to use can.

Example: Is Claudia able to go to the movies?
Can Claudia go to the movies?

1. John knows how to play the guitar. _____

2. Nga is able to speak English. _____

3. Does Jose know how to drive a car? _____

4. Marta may play with the children today. _____

_____

5. Ludmilla is sick today. She <u>is unable to</u> go to work. _____

_____

6. Nelson <u>does not know know how to</u> play tennis. _____

7. <u>Are</u> you <u>able to</u> tell me my marks? _____

8. <u>Do</u> they <u>know how to</u> swim? _____

9. Where <u>am</u> I <u>able to</u> cash a cheque? _____

10. I am so tired so I <u>am not able to</u> study now. _____

_____

I. Change <u>can</u> to <u>could</u> and make any other changes necessary in the above sentences.

_____

_____

_____

_____

_____

_____

_____

_____

_____

_____

_____

_____

_____

Model Composition

Quebec

From 1608 until 1763, the government of New France was French. During this period there were five wars with the English and two with the Indians. In 1763 the province of New France was renamed Quebec.

In 1867 the British North America Act was adopted. This started Canadian Confederation. It divided the power between the central government and the provincial governments of Nova Scotia, New Brunswick, Ontario and Quebec. These four provinces joined the Confederation of Canada at this time.

Although many Canadians of French origin live in other provinces, Quebec is the heart of French culture in Canada today.

Questions:

1. When was the government of New France French? _____

_____

2. How many wars were there from 1608 to 1763? _____

_____

3. When was the British North America Act adopted? _____

_____

4. What did Confederation do? _____

_____

5. What provinces joined the Confederation of Canada in 1867? _____

_____

6. Where is the heart of French culture today? _____

_____

Write a composition about culture in <u>your</u> country.

_____

_____

_____

_____

_____

_____

_____

_____

_____

_____

_____

_____

_____

_____

_____

_____

_____

_____

Unit VII

Past Tense Irregular Verbs, Question Words, Common Irregular Verbs

A. Rewrite each sentence using the past tense of the verbs given.

1. I mailed the letter to her last week.

   take _____

   write _____

   bring _____

   send _____

2. She cycled to Edmonton yesterday.

   drive _____

   fly _____

   go _____

   ride _____

3. We cooked dinner at eight last night.

   eat _____

   make _____

   begin _____

   have _____

4. They visited their friends in the park.

   find _____

   see _____

   leave _____

   meet _____

B. Rewrite the entire sentence, adding the past tense of the verb in parentheses.

1. She _____ the letter last week. (read) _____

_____

2. You _____ the baby in your arms. (hold) _____

_____

3. The children _____ together in the choir. (sing) _____

_____

4. The dog _____ the burglar on the arm. (bite) _____

_____

5. We _____ the word in our dictionary. (find) _____

_____

6. Jack _____ with her last week. (speak) _____

_____

7. We _____ coffee for them last night. (make) _____

_____

8. Sandra _____ in front of Bob yesterday. (sit) _____

_____

9. I _____ my homework last night. (do) _____

_____

C. Change every day to yesterday.

1. She speaks English every day. _____

2. We sleep until noon every day. _____

3. John and I do the dishes every day. _____

_____

4. You take the bus to school every day. _____

_____

5. I leave the house at nine every day. _____

_____

6. Mr. Colins sits in the back row every day. _____

_____

7. Susan knows the answers every day. _____

_____

8. The dog brings the man his slippers every day. _____

_____

9. The class begins at eight every day. _____

_____

10. The sun comes up every day. _____

D. Rewrite the entire sentence, adding the correct form of the required verbs.

1. The alarm usually rings at seven o'clock, but yesterday it _____ at eight. _____

_____

_____

2. I usually begin my work at nine, but yesterday I _____ at noon. _____

_____

_____

3. We usually swim in the pool, but last week we _____ in the lake. _____

_____

_____

4. They usually choose popular music, but last Sunday they _____ classical. _____

_____

_____

5. The wind usually blows at night, but yesterday it _____ all morning. _____

_____

_____

6. You usually do your homework well, but last week you _____ it badly. _____

_____

_____

7. He usually drinks milk for breakfast, but yesterday he _____ juice. _____

_____

_____

8. We usually speak English in class, but yesterday we _____ French. _____

_____

_____

E. Rewrite the following sentences in the negative.

Example: She ate fish last night.
She didn't eat fish last night.

1. He went to Vancouver last week. _____

_____

2. George came to class on time yesterday. _____

_____

3. I put the letter in your mailbox. _____

_____

4. You made many mistakes in your test. _____

_____

5. They bought their furniture second-hand. _____

_____

6. You knew the answers. _____

7. We sang Christmas carols last year. _____

_____

8. I thought about it last night. _____

_____

9. He slept in yesterday morning. _____

_____

10. They read their lessons before class. _____

_____

F. Rewrite the sentences above in the interrogative.

Example: *She ate fish last night.*
               Did she eat fish last night?

_____

_____

_____

_____

_____

_____

_____

_____

_____

_____

_____

_____

_____

_____

_____

_____

_____

_____

G. Rewrite the following paragraph, changing <u>every year</u> to <u>last year</u>.

Every year on my birthday, I have a party. I invite all my friends. They come to my house in the evening. We listen to music, dance, talk, play games and eat. My mother makes me a big birthday cake. I blow out all the candles and my friends sing "Happy Birthday" to me. Many friends bring me birthday presents. Everyone has a good time.

_____

_____

_____

_____

_____

_____

_____

H. Write a paragraph by answering the following questions affirmatively. (Do not begin each sentence with <u>yes</u>.)

Did you eat out last Saturday night? Did you go to a fine restaurant with your friend? Did you leave the house at seven-thirty and drive to your friend's house? Did you arrive at the restaurant at eight o'clock? Was the reservation for eight? Did the waiter take you to your table? Did you have cocktails before the meal? Did you order fish? Did your friend order coq au vin? Did you drink wine with your dinner? Were you too full to eat dessert? Did you have a good time there?

_____

_____

_____

_____

_____

_____

_____

_____

I. Crossword Puzzle
Put the answer in the past tense.

ACROSS
2. drive
4. read
6. sell
8. begin
10. feel
11. get
12. catch
14. speak
15. think
17. find
20. are
22. eat
23. write
24. see
25. leave
26. say
27. send

DOWN
1. give
3. ride
5. win
6. sing
7. sleep
9. take
10. freeze
12. choose
13. hit
14. shine
16. grow
18. deal
19. make
20. go
21. tell

J. Rewrite the entire sentence, adding a question word.

1. _____ is your name? _____

2. _____ old are you? _____

3. _____ do you live? _____

4. _____ do you do? _____

5. _____ teaches you English? _____

6. _____ color are your eyes? _____

7. _____ is that pretty girl? _____

8. _____ is your book? _____

9. _____ pen is this? _____

10. _____ is yours, the red coat or the blue one? _____

_____

11. _____ makes milk sour? _____

12. _____ are you doing now? _____

13. _____ understands this word? _____

14. _____ composition is yours? _____

15. _____ is your telephone number? _____

16. _____ shoes are these? _____

17. _____ do you spell "dictionary"? _____

18. _____ did you arrive so late? _____

19. _____ are you going this week-end? _____

20. _____ is your birthday? _____

K. Make questions for these sentences.

Example: *I study English in Canada.*
                Where do you study English?
                What do you study in Canada?

1. You lived in Calgary last year.

   Who _____

   Where _____

   When _____

2. Joan is coming here to help us.

   Who _____

   Why _____

3. Mrs. Anderson teaches you English on Mondays.

   Who _____

_____

   What _____

_____

When _____

_____

4. He was born in 1954 in Canada.

When _____

Where _____

5. I came to school by bus yesterday.

How _____

When _____

6. They buy shoes in the department store.

What _____

Where _____

7. She likes Andrew's car because it's new.

Whose _____

Why _____

8. Bill likes the red car best.

Which _____

Who _____

9. We have five toes on each foot.

How many _____

Where _____

What _____

10. My car cost $3000 two years ago.

What _____

How much _____

When _____

11. Sylvia goes to college in Quebec.

Who _____

Where _____

12. Mary practices the piano several times a day.

How often _____

What _____

13. My husband went to school for eighteen years.

Who _____

Where _____

How long _____

14. She failed the test because she didn't study.

Why _____

15. Mr. Tate's house has ten rooms.

Whose _____

How many _____

L. Make a question about the underlined words.

Example: *It's ten o'clock.*
What time is it?

1. He usually gets up at eight o'clock. _____

_____

2. They have three cars. _____

3. I live on Underhill Drive. _____

4. John takes the bus to work. _____

5. He takes the Elbow Drive bus. _____

6. I go downtown every Saturday. _____

7. He went to Calgary last week. _____

8. Sally opened the window. _____

9. The dog is ten years old. _____

10. Bob goes to the movies once a week. _____

_____

11. They went to Anna's house. _____

12. The men worked in Toronto. _____

13. There were ten people in the room. _____

_____

14. She was born on May 2. _____

15. The teachers need a holiday. _____

16. I cleaned the house all morning. _____

_____

17. They were early because the roads were good. _____

18. He gave me his father's hat. _____

19. We put <u>the books</u> in the briefcase. _____

_____

20. She went home <u>to have lunch</u>. _____

21. I want <u>the black</u> shoes. _____

22. They came to Canada <u>by airplane</u>. _____

23. <u>Barbara</u> knows the answers. _____

A Driver's License

When you apply for a driver's license, you have to pass a written test and a driving test. You must demonstrate that you are a careful driver and that you know the rules of the road.

Can you recognize the following road signs? What does each one mean?

Model Composition

My First Day

I remember my first day in Canada very well. My plane landed at Toronto Airport on an afternoon in December. It was very cold. My friends met me and we took the airport limousine to my hotel. On the way, I saw the tall buildings of the downtown area of the city. After my friends left, I unpacked my suitcase and then went out. I decided to go to a store to buy a pair of walking shoes. I stopped a man and asked where there was a shoe store. He asked me to repeat what I had said, and then put me on a large bus. I had no idea where I was going. Finally, the bus stopped at the zoo! I must have said "zoo" instead of "shoe".

I returned to the hotel and went to bed. I was very tired but couldn't get to sleep. I lay in bed and decided to begin learning English right away.

Questions:

1. Where did your plane land? _____

_____

2. How was the weather? _____

_____

3. How did you get to your hotel? _____

_____

4. What did you see on the way? _____

_____

5. What did you do after your friends left? _____

_____

6. What did you decide to do? _____

_____

7. What did you ask the man? _____

_____

8. Where did the bus stop? _____

_____

9. Why did you end up at the zoo? _____

_____

10. What did you decide to do as you lay in bed? _____

_____

Write a composition about your first day in Canada, following the model.

_____

_____

Common Irregular Verbs

Simple Form	Past	Past Participle	Simple Form	Past	Past Participle
be	was, were	been	know	knew	known
beat	beat	beaten	lay	laid	laid
become	became	become	lead	led	led
begin	began	begun	learn	learned (learnt)	learned (learnt)
bend	bent	bent	leave	left	left
bite	bit	bitten	lend	lent	lent
blow	blew	blown	lie	lay	lain
break	broke	broken	lose	lost	lost
bring	brought	brought	make	made	made
build	built	built	mean	meant	meant
burn	burned (burnt)	burned (burnt)	meet	met	met
buy	bought	bought	pay	paid	paid
catch	caught	caught	put	put	put
choose	chose	chosen	read	read	read
come	came	come	ride	rode	ridden
cost	cost	cost	ring	rang	rung
cut	cut	cut	run	ran	run
deal	dealt	dealt	say	said	said
dig	dug	dug	see	saw	seen
do	did	done	sell	sold	sold
draw	drew	drawn	send	sent	sent
dream	dreamed (dreamt)	dreamed (dreamt)	set	set	set
drink	drank	drunk	shine	shone	shone
drive	drove	driven	show	showed	shown
eat	ate	eaten	shut	shut	shut
fall	fell	fallen	sing	sang	sung
feed	fed	fed	sink	sank	sunk
feel	felt	felt	sit	sat	sat
fight	fought	fought	sleep	slept	slept
find	found	found	speak	spoke	spoken
fly	flew	flown	spend	spent	spent
forget	forgot	forgotten	stand	stood	stood
freeze	froze	frozen	steal	stole	stolen
get	got	got (gotten)	stick	stuck	stuck
give	gave	given	sweep	swept	swept
go	went	gone	swim	swam	swum
grow	grew	grown	take	took	taken
hang	hung	hung	teach	taught	taught
have	had	had	tear	tore	torn
hear	heard	heard	tell	told	told
hide	hid	hidden	throw	threw	thrown
hit	hit	hit	understand	understood	understood
hold	held	held	wake	woke	woken
hurt	hurt	hurt	wear	wore	worn
keep	kept	kept	weep	wept	wept
			win	won	won
			wind	wound	wound
			write	wrote	written

Unit VIII

Count/Non-Count (Mass) Nouns

A. Rewrite the entire sentence in the negative.

Example: I have a lot of money.
I don't have much money.

1. They write many letters every week. _____

_____

2. We needed some milk. _____

3. Does he drink much water? _____

4. You have a lot of friends in the snack bar. _____

_____

5. I made some mistakes on my test. _____

_____

6. John had little difficulty with English. _____

_____

7. Susan baked many pies for dinner. _____

_____

8. There were few people there. _____

9. I drank some coffee yesterday. _____

10. Dogs need lots of food. _____

B. Rewrite the entire sentence in the interrogative.

Example: I have a lot of money.
Do you have much money?

1. Jane knows lots of restaurants in Halifax. _____

_____

2. I bought some bread yesterday for breakfast. _____

_____

3. We understand a little English. _____

_____

4. You attend a few lectures. _____

5. Restaurant employees wash lots of dishes every day. _____

_____

6. Bob needs some help with chemistry. _____

_____

7. There is a little money in my purse. _____

_____

8. She saw many people at the drive-in. _____

_____

9. I don't wear much jewelry. _____

_____

10. They found some oil on his property. _____

_____

C. Write a paragraph by answering the following questions.

Did you buy any groceries last week? Did you buy much meat? Did you buy any fish? Did you buy any oranges? Did you buy much bread? Did you buy any eggs? Did you buy any cheese? Did you buy much fruit? Did you buy any wine in the grocery store?

_____

_____

_____

_____

_____

_____

D. Write the following paragraph so that the meaning is opposite.

Jane doesn't have much money. She also doesn't have much time. She doesn't go shopping very often. She doesn't buy many clothes or jewelry. She doesn't have many pairs of shoes and she doesn't buy any more. She doesn't buy any hats. She buys some food and a few books. She doesn't buy much furniture. Jane buys a lot of medicine because she has a lot of problems with her health.

_____

_____

_____

_____

_____

_____

_____

_____

_____

E. Rewrite the entire sentence, adding some form of <u>some</u> or <u>any</u>.

1. She didn't say _____ to me about it. _____

_____

2. We haven't got _____ wine. _____

3. She lives _____ on Fourteenth Street. _____

_____

4. The police found him _____ in Saskatchewan. _____

_____

5. I hear _____ in the kitchen. _____

6. Isn't there _____ who likes beer? _____

_____

7. Would you like _____ tea? _____

8. _____ wants to see you. _____

9. Does he have _____ money? _____

10. Would you like _____ to eat? _____

11. Margaret has _____ very pretty blouses. _____

_____

12. I don't know _____ who can speak Russian. _____

_____

13. Don't they want to do _____? _____

14. I'm certain that my pen is _____ in my purse. _____

_____

15. I learned _____ new words today. _____

_____

16. He looked but he didn't see the coffee _____. _____

_____

17. We never make _____ mistakes. _____

18. Lee doesn't have _____ to talk to. _____

19. She needs to talk to _____ . _____

20. James wants to buy her _____ different for Christmas. _____

F. Answer the following questions in complete sentences.

1. Do you have any change in your pocket? _____

2. Are there any Germans in this class? _____

3. Is there anyone behind you? _____

4. Did you make any mistakes on your last test? _____

5. Do you know anyone in Regina? _____

6. Are you going anywhere for Christmas? _____

7. Did you study anything last night? _____

8. Do you have any pets? _____

9. Do you know anything about Canadian politics? _____

10. Are there any books on your desk? _____

G. Choose the correct expression on the left of the sentence to fill in the blank.

Example: *a few, lots of*   *I have _____ time.*
                                     I have lots of time.

1. a, some   Please have _____ milk.

2. much, many   There are _____ people in the world.

3. this, lots of   _____ boy likes football better than skiing.

4. a few, much   Do you have _____ pennies?

5. a good deal of, many   They need _____ bricks to build a house.

6. any, another   Does Helen want _____ help?

7. a little, many   Mariati is buying _____ fruit.

8. each, a lot of   The teacher gives a test to _____ student.

9. many, enough   Is there _____ time left?

10. neither, all the   _____ boys were happy.

Model Composition

Resources in Canada

Canada is a land of splendid resources. Coal is mined in Nova Scotia, nickel-copper ore in Ontario and the copper mine in Manitoba is one of the greatest in the world. Gold is still found in Canada as well as nickel, asbestos, platinum and radium. In addition, there is a great deal of oil. This is found mainly in Alberta, where approximately 90 percent of the oil and natural gas for the whole of Canada is produced.

Canada is famous as an agricultural country. It produces grain in the Prairie Provinces, dairy products in Quebec and Ontario, and fruit in the orchards of Nova Scotia and British Columbia. In southern Alberta, there is grazing land for huge herds of cattle.

Lumber is an important product too, and the pulp and paper industry is one of the largest. The great Niagara Falls provide cheap hydro-electric power and the pure cold waters of Canada have long been known for their fisheries.

Questions:

1. Name some of Canada's resources which are mined. _____

_____

2. Where is most of the oil found? _____

_____

3. Where is grain produced? Dairy products? Fruit? _____

_____

_____

4. What is there in southern Alberta? _____

_____

5. How do Niagara Falls help Canada? _____

_____

6. What are the pure cold waters of Canada known for? _____

_____

Write a composition telling about the resources of <u>your</u> country.

_____

_____

_____

_____

_____

_____

_____

_____

_____

_____

_____

_____

_____

_____

_____

_____

_____

_____

_____

_____

_____

_____

_____

_____

_____

_____

_____

_____

Crossword Puzzle

Count and Non-Count Words

	ACROSS
1.	coins
4.	including two
7.	opposite of "some"
8.	space
10.	not many
13.	part of verb "to be"
14.	past tense "has"
16.	life, vitality
17.	negative word
19.	what the postman brings
21.	steak, porkchops, etc.
22.	quite a large number
23.	word with "neither"
25.	possessive adjective
26.	time when you are young
29.	suggestions, assistance
30.	not too much, not too little

	DOWN
2.	important stories
3.	every one
4.	near
5.	minutes, hours, etc.
6.	politeness
9.	modal expressing possibility, might
11.	this but not that
12.	same as #7 across
15.	a good _____ of
18.	all, used with singular nouns
19.	lots of
20.	not too much
22.	a number of
24.	opposite of "a little"
25.	dirty water
27.	"a" or "an"
28.	opposite of "yes"

Unit IX

Articles

A. Rewrite the entire sentence, adding <u>the</u> if required.

Example: *She comes from _____ United States.*
She comes from the United States.

1. He goes to _____ school at eight every day. _____

_____

2. _____ children like candy. _____

3. _____ sun shone brightly yesterday. _____

_____

4. French people like _____ wine. _____

5. _____ wine that I like isn't for sale. _____

_____

6. _____ front door is open. _____

7. Come to _____ office after lunch. _____

_____

8. _____ Prime Minister lives in Ottawa. _____

_____

9. What is _____ weather like today? _____

_____

10. _____ dog that belongs to John is in the park. _____

_____

11. _____ dogs like _____ bones. _____

12. _____ English is difficult for me. _____

13. _____ Lebanon is in _____ Middle East. _____

_____

14. _____ holidays are very relaxing. _____

15. He went to _____ bed at midnight. _____

16. She is studying _____ French. _____

17. When are you going _____ home? _____

18. I eat _____ lunch in the cafeteria. _____

19. _____ coffee isn't good for _____ sick people. _____

20. _____ babies like _____ milk. _____

21. Bob lives on _____ Seventeenth Avenue. _____

22. _____ Canada is a large country. _____

23. _____ tea you made tastes funny. _____

24. I like to eat _____ bread and _____ butter. _____

25. _____ kitchen in our house is very large. _____

26. _____ Spanish language is easy to learn. _____

27. Susan likes _____ wine better than _____ beer. _____

28. _____ blondes have more fun. _____

29. Let's drive along _____ Centre Street. _____

30. _____ Mrs. Anderson comes from _____ England. _____

31. Turn on _____ radio. _____

32. _____ class is cancelled today. _____

B. Fill in the blanks with <u>a</u>, <u>an</u>, <u>the</u> or <u>x</u>. <u>x</u> means that no article is needed.

After _____ school today, I'm going _____ home. My family usually has _____ dinner at _____ six o'clock. I must hurry because we live on _____ Seventy-Sixth Street and that is far from _____ school I attend. I usually take _____ Southpark bus to get home. Sometimes I get _____ ride with _____ boy who sits in front of me in class.

I worked very hard at _____ school today and I feel quite tired. I think I'll go to _____ bed before midnight tonight. Perhaps tomorrow I'll finish reading _____ book I started last week. I don't have to get up early tomorrow because it is _____ Sunday. However, I must get out of _____ bed, go to _____ church and have _____ lunch at my grandmother's house, as usual.

C. Fill in the blanks with a, an, the or x. x means that no article is needed.

I received many presents at Christmas. My mother gave me _____ new dress. _____ dress is red with gold buttons. My father gave me _____ book that I had asked him to buy me. I got _____ lot of small things, like _____ dozen pairs of _____ stockings, and _____ few handkerchiefs.

After Christmas my parents and I took _____ month's vacation. We went to _____ Italy and _____ Middle East. We were going to go to _____ Sweden and _____ Denmark, but _____ weather is too cold there. My favorite season is _____ summer and _____ sun is warm in _____ Italy in _____ January.

We visited the city of Milano in _____ Italy. It is such _____ beautiful city. We attended _____ opera and went to _____ movies several times. Most of _____ people were very friendly. We met _____ student who invited us to his home for _____ lunch. It was _____ excellent lunch. After lunch his family went to _____ bed. He did not want to stay at _____ home. It was _____ Sunday and he did not have to go to _____ class. He wanted to go with us to _____ church. _____ church was on _____ Fifth Avenue, so we took _____ Fifth Avenue bus. On the way we saw _____ children playing in _____ streets, _____ women talking with neighbors, and _____ men talking to other men. _____ men were talking about _____ most important news of _____ day.

After _____ church we went to have _____ supper as it was _____ seven o'clock. We were very tired after _____ supper and so we went back to _____ hotel to _____ bed.

D. Rewrite the following paragraph, adding a, an and the where necessary.

Last week I bought new dress. Dress is red with white buttons. I bought dress in department store on Eighth Avenue.

On my way home I stopped at Safeway on Elbow Drive. I needed to buy dozen eggs, meat and oranges. Meat cost $4.00 pound and eggs cost $2.50 per dozen. I bought dollar's worth of oranges.

It was such cold day that I decided to go home. Worst thing happened to me. My apartment is on one of top floors and elevator was broken. I had to walk upstairs. As soon as I had eaten supper, I went to bed because I was so tired.

_____

_____

_____

_____

_____

_____

_____

_____

_____

_____

_____

_____
_____
_____
_____
_____
_____
_____
_____
_____

Model Composition

Royal Canadian Mounted Police

The Canadian Government organized the RCMP in 1873. At that time it sent 300 men to the West to establish law and order there and to prevent fighting among the Native peoples. Because they respected the red-coated British soldiers, the police chose that color for their uniform.

In 1878, the Mounties first used the Musical Ride, where 32 men and horses perform a variety of movements to music. Around the world, nearly a million people see the Musical Ride each year.

Questions:

1. When was the RCMP organized? _____

_____

2. Who organized them? _____

_____

3. Where were the 300 men sent? _____

_____

4. Why were they organized? _____

_____

5. Why did they choose a bright red coat as part of their uniform? _____

_____

6. When did the Mounties first use the Musical Ride? _____

_____

7. What is the Musical Ride? _____

_____

8. How many people see it each year? _____

_____

Unit X

Prepositions

A. Rewrite the entire sentence, adding <u>in</u>, <u>on</u> or <u>at</u> in time phrases.

1. We are leaving _____ Wednesday _____ three o'clock _____ the afternoon. _____

_____

_____

2. My birthday is _____ July 18. _____

3. I finished school _____ May, 1973. _____

_____

4. My plane landed _____ Toronto airport _____ June 5. _____

_____

5. The course begins _____ Monday _____ eight o'clock _____ the morning. _____

_____

_____

6. We did lesson six _____ Friday. _____

7. They rented the house _____ December 15. _____

_____

8. Do you get up _____ noon every day? _____

_____

9. We often go out _____ the evenings. _____

_____

10. Hallowe'en is _____ October. _____

11. We take our holidays _____ the summer. _____

_____

12. Columbus discovered America _____ 1492. _____

_____

13. The moon shines _____ night. _____

14. World War II began _____ 1939 and ended _____ 1945. _____

_____

15. The leaves fall from the trees _____ the fall. _____

_____

B. Rewrite the entire sentence, adding <u>in</u>, <u>on</u> or <u>at</u> in place phrases.

1. I live _____ Edmonton. _____

2. The house is _____ 8th Avenue. _____

   _____

3. My parents live _____ 628-9th St. _____

   _____

4. Germany is _____ Europe. _____

5. They worked _____ a farm last summer. _____

   _____

6. Let's take a walk _____ the country. _____

   _____

7. I dropped my book _____ the floor. _____

   _____

8. When we're in Kingston we stay _____ the Moose Inn. ____

   _____

9. When it's cold we stay _____ the house. _____

   _____

10. I am studying _____ Simon Fraser University. _____

    _____

11. She always sits _____ the first row. _____

    _____

12. My mother is never _____ home on Saturdays. _____

    _____

C. Rewrite the entire sentence, adding <u>near</u>, <u>by</u> or <u>with</u>.

1. We go to work _____ bus. _____

2. Is there anything wrong _____ your stove? _____

   _____

3. What's the matter _____ Andrew? _____

   _____

4. Do you make all your clothes _____ hand? _____

   _____

5. They like to travel _____ car. _____

6. My grandfather walks _____ a cane. _____

_____

7. Mary often eats lunch _____ us. _____

_____

8. I sit in the living room _____ myself. _____

_____

D. Rewrite the entire sentence, adding <u>from</u>, <u>to</u> or <u>for</u>.

1. We were early _____ class yesterday. _____

_____

2. What did you eat _____ breakfast? _____

_____

3. The Smiths live across the street _____ us. _____

_____

4. Give this key _____ Sandra, please. _____

_____

5. Do you like _____ listen _____ classical music? _____

_____

6. He asked his friend _____ a loan. _____

_____

7. I run home _____ school every day. _____

_____

8. We are flying _____ Montreal in June. _____

_____

9. I don't need any advice _____ you. _____

_____

10. Paolo thanked me _____ the gift. _____

_____

E. Rewrite the entire sentence, filling in the blanks with <u>near</u>, <u>by</u>, <u>with</u>, <u>before</u>, <u>after</u>, <u>to</u>, <u>from</u> or <u>for</u>.

1. They went to Saskatoon _____ bus. _____

_____

2. Sally has lunch _____ her husband every day. _____

3. Monday comes _____ Tuesday. _____

4. Julie comes _____ England. _____

5. Bryan sits _____ the wall. _____

6. September comes _____ August. _____

7. We are going _____ South America _____ visit some friends. _____

8. I worked in Paris _____ a year. _____

9. A lot of shoes are made _____ machine. _____

10. What do you eat _____ lunch? _____

11. Come over _____ our house next week. _____

12. She waited _____ an hour _____ the bus. _____

13. Mary asked the teacher _____ some help. _____

14. The shopping centre is _____ my apartment. _____

15. They often go _____ a drink after work. _____

16. I'm expecting a telephone call _____ David. _____

17. The teacher was early and arrived _____ the class began. _____

18. The baby eats _____ a spoon, not _____ a fork. _____

19. Children go back to school _____ the holidays. _____

20. You clean your sidewalk _____ a shovel in the winter. _____

F. Rewrite the following paragraph, adding the required preposition. (Choose from <u>at</u>, <u>in</u>, <u>from</u>, <u>on</u> or <u>near</u>.)

Amy comes _____ Hong Kong. She arrived _____ Canada _____ March 22, 1998. She is living _____ Vancouver now. Her apartment is _____ Harwood Street _____ the Lion's Gate Bridge. She lives _____ 422 Morley Court.

Now rewrite the above paragraph, substituting "I" for "Amy". (Make other changes so that your paragraph is true for you.)

_____

_____

_____

_____

_____

_____

G. Rewrite the following paragraphs, adding the required prepositions. (Choose from <u>in</u>, <u>at</u>, <u>to</u>, <u>near</u>, <u>on</u>, <u>by</u>, <u>with</u>, <u>for</u> or <u>before</u>.)

Miss Bennett goes _____ work _____ nine o'clock. She works _____ a bank. The bank is _____ her apartment so she walks _____ work every morning. Her apartment is _____ 8th Avenue and the bank is _____ 163-8th Avenue.

After work she goes _____ bus _____ the Y.W.C.A. She swims and exercises _____ an hour _____ dinner. She has dinner _____ the Y.W.C.A. _____ some of her friends.

_____

_____

_____

_____

_____

_____

_____

_____

_____

_____

_____

H. Answer the following questions in complete sentences, using the information in parentheses. Insert the article where necessary.

Example: When do you eat lunch? (noon)
I eat lunch at noon.

1. Where do you live? (Fredericton) _____

2. When do Canadians ski? (winter) _____

3. When is your anniversary? (July 18) _____

_____

4. When did you buy your rug? (March) _____

_____

5. When were you born? (1955) _____

6. Where do you live? (784 Mason Drive) _____

_____

7. Where are your shoes? (feet) _____

8. When do you do your homework? (night) _____

_____

9. When did you paint the ceiling? (Tuesday) _____

_____

10. Where is the bus stop? (corner) _____

11. Where is your key? (pocket) _____

12. Where do you shower? (bathroom) _____

13. Where is the table? (kitchen) _____

14. Where do you find new words? (dictionary) _____

_____

15. What are you listening to? (stereo) _____

_____

16. What are you looking for? (front door) _____

_____

17. What are you waiting for? (elevator) _____

_____

18. Who is the parcel from? (Andrew) _____

19. Where was your mother born? (Nova Scotia) _____

_____

20. Where do you come from? (Spain) _____

21. How long were you at school yesterday? (five hours) _____

_____

22. How do you go to work? (car) _____

23. What do you write with? (pencil) _____

I. Fill in the blanks with <u>in</u>, <u>from</u>, <u>on</u>, <u>at</u>. Then answer each question.

1. What country do you come _____? _____

2. What country do you live _____? _____

3. What city do you live _____? _____

4. What street do you live _____? _____

5. What number do you live _____? _____

6. What village were you born _____? _____

7. What month were you born _____? _____

8. What hospital were you born _____? _____

9. What day were you born _____? _____

J. Make questions about the underlined words.

1. I come <u>from Quebec</u>. _____

2. Mary was born <u>in Germany</u>. _____

3. Her birthday is <u>in July</u>. _____

4. He went to bed <u>at midnight</u>. _____

5. They go to school <u>by bus</u>. _____

6. The teacher lives <u>on Greenview Road</u>. _____

7. John eats <u>pie</u> for breakfast every day. _____

_____

8. Mrs. Colins makes all her clothes <u>by hand</u>. _____

_____

9. They play cards <u>with us</u> every Friday. _____

_____

10. <u>New Year's Day</u> comes after Christmas. _____

_____

Model Composition

Our Home

We live in a house in town. There are three bedrooms upstairs and there is a bathroom there too.

On the main floor we have another small bathroom, a kitchen and a living room with a dining area. In the kitchen there is a table and four chains where we can eat our breakfast and lunch. We usually have dinner in the dining room.

We have a small yard in front of the house and a large garden behind the house. There are a lot of trees and flowers in our garden and we also grow some vegetables there every summer.

Write a short composition about where you live following the model above.

_____ _____

_____

_____

_____

_____

_____

_____

_____

_____

_____

_____

_____

_____

_____

_____

_____

Model Composition

The First Canadians

The ancestors of North American Natives probably came from Asia across the Bering Strait thousands of years ago. Eventually they spread over most of Canada and the United States, and they developed many different languages and ways of living.

Five centuries ago there were over 200 000 Native people living in Canada. Some hunted for their food. They made all their tools and weapons from stone, bone or wood, and they lived in teepees or wigwams.

When the white men came, they brought a new way of life. The Natives taught them how to walk on snow and how to paddle canoes. The canoes greatly helped the Europeans to explore the country. But as the forests were cut down, the wildlife moved farther west and north, and many Natives died from disease brought by the new settlers.

Today, over 100 000 Native people live in Canada, many on reservations where there are special laws to protect and assist them.

Questions:

1. Where did the ancestors of the North American Natives come from? _____

_____

2. How many people were living in Canada five centuries ago? _____

_____

3. How did they make their tools? _____

_____

4. What did they live in? _____

5. What did the Natives teach the white men? _____

_____

6. How were the canoes helpful to the Europeans? _____

_____

7. What happened as the forests were cut down? _____

_____

8. Where do many Native people live today? _____

_____

Write a composition about the first people to live in your country.

_____

_____

_____

_____

_____

_____

_____

_____

_____

_____

_____

_____

Unit XI
Future

A. Change <u>every day</u> to <u>tomorrow</u>. Use the <u>will</u> form.

1. We wash our hair every day. _____

2. Sandra brushes her teeth every day. _____

_____

3. The students sit in the classroom every day. _____

_____

4. I study my lessons every day. _____

5. You and John work in the library every day. _____

_____

6. I go to work at eight every day. _____

7. The sun shines in Alberta every day. _____

_____

8. The cat washes its ears every day. _____

9. Mr. and Mrs. Anderson drink tea every day. _____

_____

10. Jack and Jill shower every day. _____

11. It rains in Vancouver every day. _____

B. Change <u>yesterday</u> to <u>next week</u>. Use the <u>going to</u> form.

1. I went to the movies yesterday. _____

_____

2. The classes began at nine yesterday. _____

_____

3. Mary and Alice spoke French yesterday. _____

_____

4. We found our friends yesterday. _____

_____

5. Martin saw two bears yesterday. _____

_____

6. They ate in the cafeteria yesterday. _____

_____

7. You rode in a train yesterday. _____

_____

8. Miss Sorenson talked to the Prime Minister yesterday. _____

_____

9. My mother cooked chicken-in-wine yesterday. _____

_____

10. I swam in Lake Erie yesterday. _____

_____

11. I flew to Regina yesterday. _____

_____

C. Rewrite the entire sentence in the interrogative.

1. We're going to leave next month. _____

_____

2. Kate will return in May. _____

3. She'll be in the bath. _____

4. They are going to Prince George tomorrow. _____

_____

5. Susan is going to have an eye examination. _____

_____

6. The final examination is on June 27. _____

_____

7. Your mouth will bleed when the dentist pulls out your tooth. _____

_____

8. The janitor will clean the blackboard tonight. _____

_____

9. I'm working at home next week. _____

_____

10. She will cut her hair later. _____

11. He says it'll snow tomorrow. _____

_____

D. Rewrite the entire sentence in the negative.

1. Robert will cut his fingernails. _____

2. They'll arrive at eight o'clock. _____

3. We are going to meet them downtown. _____

   _____

4. I'll see you next week. _____

5. The Smiths are returning from holidays on Monday. _____

   _____

6. Sally is going to buy a new coat this year. _____

   _____

7. I'll do my homework tomorrow. _____

8. The movie begins at seven o'clock tomorrow. _____

   _____

9. You're going to be sorry. _____

10. They are taking their holidays next month. _____

   _____

11. John's going to need a haircut this week. _____

   _____

E. Rewrite the following paragraph, changing every day to tomorrow. Make all necessary changes.

   Mr. Andrews gets up at seven o'clock every day. He wakes the children and then makes a cup of coffee for his wife. He showers and shaves. At 7:10 he puts on a shirt and suit, and ties his tie. He even polishes his shoes. At 7:30 he makes breakfast for the children. They eat pancakes with maple syrup and drink milk. He brushes his teeth and combs his hair. He leaves for work at 8:00, but first brings his wife breakfast in bed.

   _____

   _____

   _____

   _____

   _____

   _____

   _____

   _____

   _____

   _____

F. Write a paragraph about an imaginary vacation you are planning to take this summer. (Be sure to answer the following questions in your paragraph.)

Are you planning to take a vacation this summer? Are you going to take a trip? Where will you go? How will you travel? When will you leave? Are you planning to go alone? What will you do when you get there? How long will you be away? Will you be happy to come back here again?

_____

_____

_____

_____

_____

_____

_____

_____

Model Composition

The Inuit

Across the northern parts of Canada lived the Inuit. In summer they lived in tents. In winter they lived in igloos, which they made out of blocks of snow carefully fitted together into a dome. The soil was poor in the cold north and so they depended mainly on fishing and hunting to live.

When the white man came, the lifestyle of the Inuit changed. They began to use the kerosene stove for heating and the rifle for hunting instead of the harpoon. They still depend greatly on the seal and the caribou for food and clothing to make a living for themselves in a region too cold and bitter for most other people.

Questions:

1. Where did the Inuit live? _____

_____

2. Where did they live in summer? _____

_____

3. What did they depend on mainly to live? _____

_____

4. What happened when the white men came? _____

_____

5. What do they depend on the seal and caribou for? _____

_____

6. Why don't most other people live with the Inuit? _____

_____

Unit XII

Comparison of Adjectives/Adverbs

A. **Make 2 sentences using the given words, the first in the positive degree, the second in the comparative.**

Example: *He / old / his brother.*
He is as old as his brother.
His is older than his brother.

1. Jane/thin/her cousin. _____

_____

2. Mr. Jones/handsome/Mr. Adams. _____

_____

3. She/busy/her husband. _____

_____

4. This lesson/difficult/last one. _____

_____

5. Bob/work/good/his friend. _____

_____

6. Mary/tall/her sister. _____

_____

7. He/dress/bad/his father. _____

_____

8. They/run/quick/the children. _____

_____

B. **Rewrite the entire sentence, changing the adjective or adverb from positive to comparative degree.**

Example: *He is as nice as his brother.*
He is nicer than his brother.

1. Edmonton is as cold as Saskatoon. _____

_____

2. This summer is as hot as last summer. _____

_____

3. My boots are as narrow as your shoes. _____

_____

4. That boy is as clever as his father. _____

_____

5. Sandra is as intelligent as I am. _____

_____

6. These mittens are as good as those gloves. _____

_____

7. The scarf costs as little as the hat. _____

_____

8. I play bridge as badly as my friends. _____

_____

C. Rewrite the entire sentence, changing the adjective or adverb from comparative to superlative degree.

Example: *Glenmore is bigger than any other park in Calgary.*
Glenmore is the biggest park in Calgary.

1. Your writing is better than that of any other student in the class. _____

_____

_____

2. Bill is taller than any other boy in the room. _____

_____

3. This scarf is more colorful than any other scarf on the table. _____

_____

4. My test is worse than any other test. _____

_____

5. Sally is more beautiful than any other girl in the room. _____

_____

6. Andrew studies less than any other student. _____

_____

7. This book is more useful than any other book on the shelf. _____

_____

8. Ann knows more than any other girl. _____

_____

9. The red blouse is smaller than the other blouses on the rack. _____

_____

10. She speaks more clearly than any student in the class. _____

_____

D. Rewrite the entire sentence as comparative.

Example: Judy is the same age as Margaret.
Judy is older / younger than Margaret.

1. The black shoes are the same size as the brown ones. _____

_____

2. Bryan is as intelligent as Colin. _____

_____

3. Elaine is the same height as Margaret. _____

_____

4. The mushroom soup is as good as the clam chowder. _____

_____

5. The beginning class starts the same time as the advanced class. _____

_____

6. She understands as little as I do. _____

_____

7. George dresses as carefully as Gordon does. _____

_____

8. He drives the same speed as I do. _____

_____

9. This underwear costs as much as that. _____

_____

10. Kevin is as handsome as David. _____

_____

E. Rewrite the entire sentence, adding either <u>good</u> or <u>well</u>.

Example: Mary is a <u>good</u> girl.
She writes very <u>well</u>.

1. Anthony always polishes his shoes _____. _____

_____

2. How are you? Very _____ thank you. _____

_____

3. Joan is a _____ person. _____

_____

4. She does everything _____. _____

_____

5. Is Eleanor a _____ doctor? _____

_____

6. She drives a car very _____. _____

_____

7. Janice speaks English _____. _____

_____

8. Ellen was ill but now she is _____. _____

_____

9. Janet plays chess _____. _____

10. Julia is a _____ dancer. _____

11. Am I a _____ English teacher? _____

_____

12. Joseph wants to write _____ English. _____

_____

13. She speaks it very _____. _____

_____

14. The concert was very _____ last night. _____

_____

15. You can live _____ here. _____

_____

16. David plays the guitar very _____. _____

_____

17. Peggy is a _____ student. _____

_____

18. Do you think Henry sings _____. _____

_____

19. That was a _____ horse. _____

_____

20. It ran the race _____. _____

_____

Describing Someone

Vocabulary:	arm	redhead	orange	plump	pants
face	shoulder	grey	white	slim	shorts
forehead	hand	pale	straight	thick	skirt
eyes	leg	dark	curly	round	dress
eyebrows	knee	tanned	wavy	oval	socks
eyelashes	feet	freckled	soft	square	pantyhose
nose	chest	blue	hard	triangular	shoes
cheeks	back	brown	rough		bppts
mouth	fingers	green	tall	t-shirt	hat
lips	toes	red	short	shirt	scarf
chin	hair	pink	long	blouse	jewellery
ears	brunette	beige	thin	sweater	watch
neck	blonde	yellow	wide	sweatshirt	
				jacket	

1. Write a composition describing what the teacher is wearing and his/her physical appearance.

_____

_____

_____

_____

_____

_____

_____

_____

_____

_____

2. Compare yourself with someone else in the class with respect to clothing and physical characteristics.

_____

_____

_____

_____

_____

_____

_____

_____

_____

_____

Model Composition

Politics in Canada

According to the British North America Act of 1867, Canada is governed by the elected House of Commons, an appointed Senate and a representative of the Queen – the Governor-General. In addition, each province has an elected assembly and a Lieutenant-Governor, the Queen's representative.

Some of the better known political parties are Liberal, New Democrat (NDP), Progressive Conservative (PC), the Reform Party and the Bloc Quebecois. Members of Parliament (MPs) are elected to the House of Commons by the people across Canada. The country is divided into 301 federal electoral districts, mainly on the basis of population. The party which has the majority of seats in the House of Commons forms the Government and the leader becomes the Prime Minister.

The second branch of Parliament, the Senate, consists of 104 (but can have a maximum of 112) appointed members who give formal approval to bills passed in the House of Commons. The Governor-General gives royal assent to bills that have been approved in both Houses.

Questions:

1. What are the main political parties in Canada? _____

_____

_____

2. Who elects the MPs? _____

_____

3. How many constituencies are there in the country? _____

_____

4. How is the Government formed? _____

_____

5. Who becomes Prime Minister? _____

_____

6. What is the second branch of Parliament and what does it do? _____

_____

_____

7. How many members does it consist of? _____

_____

8. Who is the representative of the Queen and what does he/she do? _____

_____

Write a composition describing the Government in <u>your</u> country.

_____
_____
_____
_____
_____
_____
_____
_____
_____
_____
_____
_____
_____
_____
_____
_____
_____
_____
_____
_____
_____
_____
_____
_____
_____
_____

Unit XIII

Present Perfect

A. Rewrite the entire sentence in the negative. (Remember to change <u>already</u> to <u>yet</u>.)

1. We've heard that story before. _____

_____

2. Brian has already paid cash. _____

_____

3. Mary has been ill for weeks. _____

_____

4. It has become cloudy. _____

5. Edward has had a car since last year. _____

_____

6. They've bought a gallon of milk. _____

_____

7. I've met many new friends already. _____

_____

8. My mother has been to the supermarket three times this week. _____

_____

9. You've ordered a lot of gifts since September. _____

_____

10. The men have already found the dairy. _____

_____

B. Rewrite the entire sentence in the interrogative. (Remember to change <u>already</u> to <u>yet</u> and <u>never</u> to <u>ever</u>.)

1. She has never worn that dress before. _____

_____

2. I've been in a drug store many times. _____

_____

3. We have read the letter before. _____

_____

4. Bob has arrived at the bank already. _____

_____

5. The children haven't come to the bakery yet. _____

_____

6. You've paid the bill already._____

_____

7. Miss Stevens has taught English before. _____

_____

8. Gordon has worked in the credit department since October. _____

_____

9. I've never charged anything before. _____

_____

10. You have met my wife already. _____

_____

C. Rewrite the entire sentence, adding the present perfect form of the verb in parentheses.

1. I (be) in the clothing store since nine o'clock. _____

_____

2. We (do) our work this way for years. _____

_____

3. Mona (break) her leg before. _____

4. You (drive) already this car. _____

5. It (begin) just to snow. _____

6. George (find) never his books. _____

7. I (know) her since last year. _____

8. They (fly) never in a helicopter. _____

9. He (speak) to me many times before. _____

_____

10. I (ride) never a bicycle. _____

D. Rewrite the entire sentence, inserting either the present perfect or the simple past form of the verb in parentheses.

1. We (go) to the gift shop last summer. _____

_____

2. I (go) there every summer since 1970. _____

_____

3. My family (leave) Vancouver two weeks ago. _____

_____

4. They (be) on the road for ten days. _____

5. It (snow) every day for three weeks. _____

6. It (rain) a great deal yesterday. _____

7. We (study) English since December. _____

_____

8. I (study) French when I was in France last year. _____

_____

9. She (see) that play many times before. _____

_____

10. Janice (see) the movie last Saturday night. _____

_____

E. Rewrite the following paragraph, adding either the present perfect or the simple past form of the verb in parentheses.

   Margaret likes to read books about Canada. She (read) already two books since Monday. On Wednesday she (read) a book abou the Native people and on Thursday night she (begin) to read a book on the Inuit. Margaret (finish) it Friday morning. Yesterday she (start) to read about the wildlife of Canada, but she (not finish) it yet.

_____

_____

_____

_____

_____

_____

_____

_____

_____

F. Crossword Puzzle

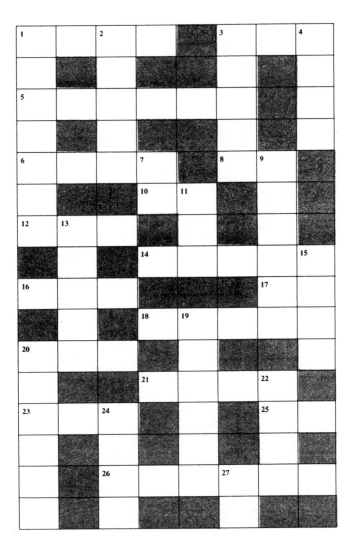

PT = Past Tense
PP = Past Participle

ACROSS
1. PT of go
3. PT of cut
5. Put in time or money for gain
6. PP of tear
8. Greeting
10. Goes with either
12. Not old
14. Preposition of time
16. PT of eat
17. Infinitive of does
18. Frequently
20. Number
21. PT of blow
23. Present of ate
25. Preposition
26. PT of land

DOWN
1. PP of write
2. Not now or ever
3. Infinitive of caught
4. PT of tell
7. Opposite of yes
9. Not outside
11. PP of run
13. PP of eat
15. Not short
19. PP of fall
20. PT of open
22. PT of wear
24. Say words, speak
27. Same as 17 across

MAP

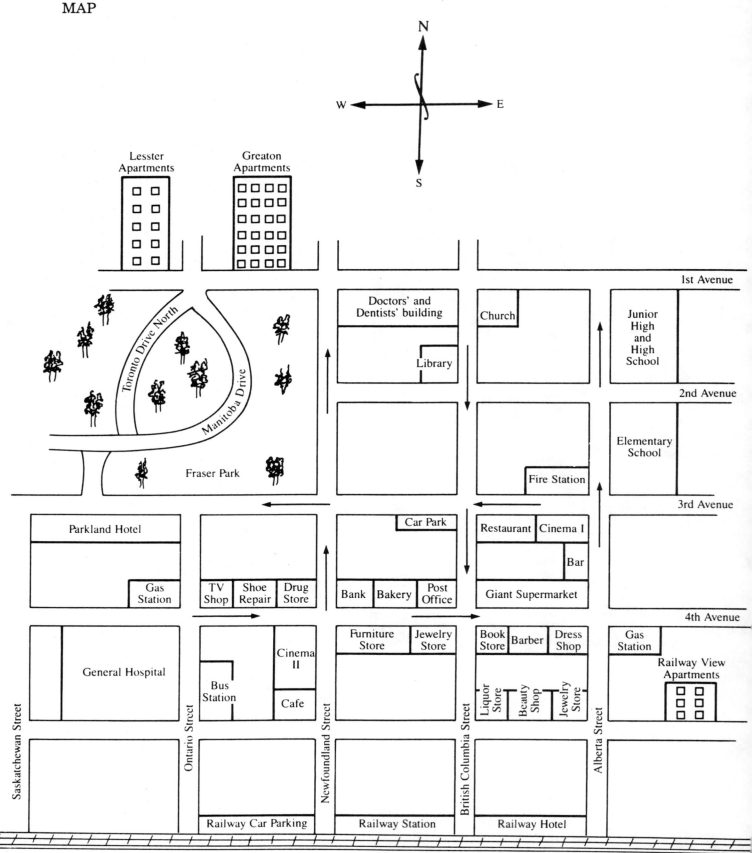

Getting About in a Small Town

Describe the routes taken below. (Remember, if you go by car, there are several one-way streets.)

1. You go by car from your apartment in the Lesster apartment building, to pick up a friend at the railway station. You take her to the Parkland Hotel and leave her there.

_____

_____

_____

_____

_____

_____

_____

2. Then you decide to go to the supermarket, the bank and the beauty shop.

_____

_____

_____

_____

_____

_____

_____

3. On the way home, you fill up the car at the gas station and stop by the library.

_____

_____

_____

_____

_____

_____

_____

_____

4. That evening, you pick up your friend in the car and take her to the restaurant for dinner. You park the car in the parking lot and after dinner you walk to Cinema II to see a movie. After the movie you walk to the cafe for a cup of coffee and then walk back to the parking lot to get the car.

_____

_____

_____

_____

_____

_____

_____

5. You drop your friend at the hotel and drive home.

_____

_____

_____

_____

_____

_____

_____

_____

Model Composition

Canadian Citizenship

If you want to become a Canadian citizen, you have to be a landed immigrant, have lived in Canada at least three years, and speak either English or French.

Also, you will have to show that you know something about the responsibilities of a Canadian citizen. You will need to have some knowledge of the geography, history, political system and the economic life in Canada.

To become a citizen you will have to take three steps: (1) make an application, (2) appear before a court for a hearing and (3) attend the court ceremony of presentation.

Questions:

1. What are the requirements if you want to become a Canadian citizen? _____

_____

_____

2. What must you show that you know about Canada? _____

_____

_____

3. What are the three steps to become a citizen? _____

_____

_____

4. Are you a landed immigrant? _____

_____

5. How many years have you lived in Canada? _____

_____

6. Do you speak French or English? _____

_____

Write what you know about the geography of Canada.

_____

_____

_____

_____

_____

_____

_____

_____

_____

_____

_____

_____

_____

_____

_____

_____

_____

_____

_____

_____

_____

_____

_____

_____

_____

_____

Write what you know about the history of Canada.

_____

_____

_____

_____

_____

_____

_____

_____

_____

_____

_____

_____

_____

_____

_____

_____

_____

_____

_____

_____

_____

_____

_____

_____

_____

_____

_____

_____

Write what you know about the political system of Canada.

_____

_____

_____

_____

_____

_____

_____

_____

_____

_____

_____

_____

_____

_____

_____

_____

_____

_____

_____

_____

_____

_____

_____

_____

_____

_____

_____

Write what you know about the economic life in Canada.

_____

_____

_____

_____

_____

_____

_____

_____

_____

_____

_____

_____

_____

_____

_____

_____

_____

_____

_____

_____

_____

_____

_____

_____

_____

_____

_____

_____

_____

_____